Softening

Also by April Green:

Bloom for Yourself
Bloom for Yourself II
Becoming a Wildflower
Reaching the Sun

Softening

Poetry and notes on becoming
who you already are.

April Green

Cover Artwork:
Xavier Esclusa Trias
www.twopots-design.com
xevi@twopots-design.com
Instagram: @xetdsgn

ISBN– 978-1-3999-3731-3

I have bloomed and
flowered
a thousand times in
this lifetime;

(even when my roots
were damaged)

because I let the dying petals fall.

Bloom for Yourself, April Green

Softening into what is

Softening into what is:

the acceptance that you are
already whole, already enough,
already unconditional love,
and you are letting go of anything
which goes against this beautiful
truth.

April Green

Love and happiness
arise within you
when you stop desiring
and expecting life
to be any different
than what it already is.

THE ART OF SURRENDER

Surrendering is not an act of doing.
Surrendering is an act of **not** doing.
Surrendering is stillness,
It is not fighting with stillness, or
trying to reach stillness.
It is **being** stillness.
It is accepting life as it is now.
It is softening into who you are now,
as you are now, so that the pain
you have been holding onto
falls away without any effort from you.
Surrendering is the freedom to move
through life
with nothing but the breath of grace
surrounding you.

April Green

The space between
whatever life is handing you
(for your highest good) and
whatever you are holding onto
causes disharmony.
But when you let go,
love and freedom will be revealed,
happiness will shine through.
You will be able to enjoy each
moment as it arrives, rather
than miss each moment because
you're holding onto what you
think will make you happy.

THE SIMPLICITY OF LIFE

The simplicity of life—*the magic, the movement, the sacred little inhales*—is obscured by the expectation for life to become something else, something more, something we can grasp and hold onto.
But when we soften into reality—when we become available to observe everything that is already here—the simplicity of life expands like a wilderness, and we see just how miraculous and breath-taking life truly is.

April Green

THE BEAUTY OF REALITY

Surrender to what life is showing you now,
for it is only in the now that beauty and joy are
revealed.

Allow everything you are witnessing to blossom
in silence, and everything will appear to you in
fullness—*the flower blooming, the birds calling, the
scent of rain.*

Within this space is the beauty of reality—a silent
observation that fills you with your own love and
well-being.

Soften into the truth.
Soften into whatever is
presently happening;
not to what you want,
or don't want
to be happening.
Soften into what life is showing you
each moment.
Soften into the way it currently is,
not the way you want it to be.

April Green

LETTING GO SITS INSIDE THE HEART OF PAIN

Each time we encounter painful emotions,
it is usually a sign that something inside us
is not being lovingly met or embraced.
The more we resist meeting our pain,
the stronger our suffering will be.

So we must try to meet our pain with compassion.
We must try to hold space for it, listen to it,
understand it, and accept that it too wants to be
free.

Only then can we let it go with grace.

April Green

Every wound: every piece of you that feels
rejected, or lonely, or unworthy, is inviting you
to start healing the deepest parts of your being.

(You deserve to carry the light instead of the weight
of pain.)

REVEALING YOUR INNER PAIN

Radical self-acceptance is necessary to be able to fully embrace and enjoy everything life is giving you. Because, once you start to welcome every single piece of who you are—the darkness, the shame, the guilt, the secrets, the pain—the Earth rises to meet you. It holds you and shows you all the different ways you can become comfortable in your own skin.

Over time, you will start to own and honour the entirety of who you are; and you will learn how to stay in this space of wholeness.

There is power, and beauty, and grace in this invitation.

MEETING YOUR PAIN

Learning to meet your pain isn't easy. But the more you do it, the more comfortable and secure you will feel. It is a tender act: you are getting to hear and learn about your deepest fears, your heaviest layers. Be curious about these shadow parts; they are here to teach you strength and resilience. If you deny and bury these parts, they will recycle around your body, and you will start expressing them in ways that are unhealthy for you.

Be gentle and loving with your unhealed pain. Meet it compassionately. Allow it to be felt and acknowledged, and then set free.

Unresolved pain has no place in the evolution of you. Just as wild roots tangled around a flower will one day suffocate its growth; so too will unresolved pain living in the earth of you.

April Green

FAITH IS TRUSTING

Faith is trusting.
It is the letting-in
that comes from letting go.
It is an opening, a breath of fresh air.
It is looking straight ahead, and not
worrying about the if or the how,
but believing that it already is.

ACCEPTANCE

There is no middle ground
when it comes to letting go.
You either identify as the person
holding on and receiving all the issues
that holding on attracts,
or you identify as the person
walking towards a new space
and welcoming all the offerings
that moving forward attracts.

You can't focus on opposing energies at the same
time; and trying to do so causes you pain and
suffering.

*Always turn towards new light—this is where you
belong.*

The stillness of your inner being
here, in every moment
sits behind any thoughts and feelings.

Rest inside the peace and unconditional love
that this space offers you until you realise
it will never abandon you.

A DANCE OF POLAR ENERGY

We think things come to stay, but really, things come to pass. And when you observe the patterns that thoughts and feelings take—*the way they rise and fall, whispering in opposites: sun and moon, Earth, and sky*—you will begin to understand the flux and flow of life; the impermanence of it all. You will begin to notice that nothing is causing you any harm unless you think it is. Everything is simply appearing as a dance of polar energy within the space of wholeness—both energies are needed to complete the whole. And no thought continues unless you give it your attention. Thoughts come, and they go on their own when you leave them alone. It is only when you cling to one side and push away the other that you suffer, because you block the flow and become stuck between the two. Once you see this movement clearly, you will learn how to breathe through any thoughts that could disturb you and move you away from who you are. Once you start welcoming each side and allow the energy to move freely, it will pass through without leaving any residue. Then, you will be able to surrender to this dance of polar energy. You will begin to accept it and celebrate the freedom of it all.

April Green

Nothing feels more serene than a soft body
surrendering to the darkness and the light.

Don't hold anything
too tightly:
no moment is better than
the one that is already here.

You are always
exactly where you need to be.

And it is beautiful.

EVERYTHING IS ALREADY WORKING FOR OUR GOOD

Greatness is always here, but we don't always recognise it—we think we need to go out and find it. And in the search, we get trapped inside an illusion of what we think greatness looks and feels like.

We confuse what life is showing us with what we want to see.

REVEALING THE HAPPINESS WITHIN

Unhealthy patterns arise from an unconscious refusal to face and move through our own pain. When people, or things come along and give us a feeling of happiness, we become attached to that feeling and believe it is caused by that person or thing. But it is not. It is the distraction from our pain that is causing us momentary happiness.

Sooner or later, the thing we keep returning to stops giving us the feeling of happiness and the pain becomes strong again. We then keep returning to this person or thing, (or find an alternative version) to try and recreate the feeling of happiness.

What we don't consciously notice is that the act of seeking, and resisting is covering over the happiness already within us, so we end up in a cycle of searching for what we already are but have failed to see.

In order to break this pattern and let go organically, we must become aware that whatever it is we are clinging to is unhealthy for us.

We must become aware that we are trapped inside a cycle of seeking pleasure and resisting pain.

April Green

We must see that we have been putting our happiness into something or someone else's hands instead of finding it within our own.

We must learn to face our pain and meet it head on. We must start the process of healing this pain and expressing it in ways that are healthy for us.

And, eventually, the happiness that is our inherent nature; (and which was being covered over by the very act of searching for it on the outside), starts breaking through our bodies like the distant sun revealing who we already are.

TRAVELING LIGHT

Give whatever is arising in your life
the total freedom to unfold fully,
*(without attempting to control it, or
manipulate it),* and you will discover
how incredibly soft life starts to feel
against your heart.

April Green

LIFE IS NOW

We miss life unfolding in front of us because we are trying to be one step ahead of life in an attempt to know it. We miss the flowers blooming beneath our feet because we are searching for the brightest, most fragrant one of all. We disconnect from the energetic flow of life because we're looking for a stronger, more colourful rainbow elsewhere. We disconnect with life because we are searching for a piece of life that gives us meaning and purpose. We leave ourselves to run ahead of ourselves, never truly softening into the state of experiencing, receiving, honouring, and serving.

We miss where the world is arising because we navigate with an external map instead of our inner compass.

We miss the beauty and the joy because our attention is focused on what we are looking *for* and not what we are looking at.

REMINDER

If you are holding onto expectations
about who you need to become,
how things should have turned out,
what you could have done differently,
what could happen next, then
you are holding up a barrier
to the life you deserve to live
now.

(Trust and believe that life always
comes together for you in the most unexpected way.)

GRACE

There is grace in everything.
When I understood this fully—
the breath, the tears, the way energy moves,
draws you in, holds you for longer than usual—
the more I honoured everything that came into
my life; even the pain.

We attach meaning to whatever appears on our path.
But the meaning comes from an echo of the past and
the projection of a future.

Grace gives nothing meaning.
Grace simply gives us love.
Grace quietly shows us the right way;
reminds us that our birthright is not to live
in tragedy, and grief and, despair.

Our birthright is to be at peace
with tragedy, and grief, and despair.

EVERY DAY IS LETTING GO

Our daily practice every day is letting go.
We don't always notice but letting go is what we do
all day: letting go of thoughts, resentments,
betrayals, and expectations: *(all the things we
wanted that didn't surface, the things we didn't want
that keep returning).*

Life is like the ocean—sometimes still, sometimes
terrifying and wild, but always moving.

Every now and again though, we turn around and
we try to hold back its flow. We stand in its way and
grasp and cling to everything slipping through our
fingers.

We fail to notice the fresh, clear water collecting
beneath our feet; the pearls of yesteryear, the
lessons, the beauty brushing against our skin.

April Green

HAVE FAITH IN NOT KNOWING

You don't need to know how something
is going to turn out.

You just need to accept that everything right now
is exactly as it should be.

Rest in this faith. Embody it.

(The desire to control outcomes blocks the right
outcome from revealing itself to you.)

April Green

LETTING GO TAKES YOU TO A HIGHER LIFE

It is frightening to let go:
to move away from the comfort and
the warmth and the familiarity
of holding on for so long.
But a beautiful life
of unconditional love
and well-being
and compassion
and freedom
is just a breath away.
I promise.
And then the pain
of holding on
will become apparent to you.
Because in the process
of surrendering, there is
a rising upwards in consciousness,
a lifting, a releasing,
before new life rushes in
to meet you.

April Green

THE BEAUTY OF NON-RESISTANCE

We don't always realise how much pain, and trauma, and resentment we are holding onto until we start to let it all go, bit by bit. But letting go cannot be forced, because forcing thoughts and feelings to leave you simply reinforces them and keeps them in your view. This is because the intention to let go gives rise to anticipation that something will happen when you let go, meaning you are still involved in an outcome. And this only serves to keep the emotional attachment to the object, or person, energetically alive.

Letting go happens organically once you surrender to what is presently happening. It happens when you reconnect with your deeper self and stop giving attention to the mental activity of what was, or what could be.

Then you just keep surrendering and softening until you are in a state of non-resistance, and acceptance.

There is nothing more beautiful than feeling the weight shifting, and the emotional stain of attachment fading like a half-remembered dream.

April Green

HOW DO YOU SURRENDER AND SOFTEN?

You sit with the feelings you are trying to be free from. You accept them as they are. You allow them to move through you without bruising you as they pass. You give them the space to slowly leave. You don't grasp them to feel them one last time. You don't pick them up to see if they've changed. You turn your attention back into yourself. You start absorbing yourself back into yourself, back into your passions, your art, your journal, your books, your music. You start finding pieces of yourself you didn't know existed. You start seeing the lessons; start noticing the gifts.

New life appears. And you nurture it.

Let pain and betrayal soften you.
Don't redirect it towards yourself.
Don't carry it within.
Sit with the discomfort of it.
Meet it.
Allow it to express itself in silence.
Only then will it move through you;
rise, and disperse like a wave with nothing
to crash into.

(You have the power to observe the flow of energy
without drowning in it.)

REMINDER

There is more action in stillness than there is
in running from yourself in search of stillness.

The only place you ever need to be
is here: home is who you already are.

WANTING CAUSES SUFFERING

Wanting what you don't have, and not having what you want are very different states.

Wanting what you don't have is the state that causes the most suffering, and it happens in the space between the **wanting** and the having. This space is perceived as separation—you have separated from the source of life because you want something your way. And once the 'having' is reached, peace and happiness arise—not because the thing you wanted has been received, but because the wanting has ceased—the agitation, the restlessness, the hunger has been relieved.

Peace, love, and happiness are your natural states, and are always there in the background; inherently free to arise, become enlivened, and absorbed. But the wanting acts as a blanket covering over these states, which leads you to believe that you need to search for them instead of seeing that you have simply separated from the source of life.

So, you must find a way to allow your natural states to re-surface. You must reconnect with yourself and **be** where you already are.

April Green

You will find your way
when you stop looking
in the distance and
start looking at the little
fragments of light beneath
your feet.

April Green

BE FULLY HERE

When your mind is given the space to breathe and untangle itself from the mental activity of the ego, (which is always narrating and interpreting what it believes to be happening), what you are left with is reality. And reality is extraordinary when you have clarity of mind because clarity is a space in which you can be fully here, and completely available.

When you soften into yourself, reality expands and softens around you like a warm embrace.

ALIGNMENT

Alignment isn't something you go out and find.
You don't have to look for it or travel anywhere
outside of yourself to reach it.

You are already aligned; you just don't always feel it
because there are too many things in the way, too
many things holding you back—the limiting beliefs,
the garments of the past, the pain.

Alignment is a rising up, a shifting in consciousness,
rather than a movement in a certain direction.

When you start doing the daily work of removing
the barriers to being aligned, you will start to feel a
sense of graceful, etheric ease; a lightness to your
life. You will be free to receive the ever-present flow
of well-being and love from the source. You will be
in alignment.

*You deserve to witness your life falling perfectly into
line.*

NATURE'S WAY

Sometimes, pain gives you no choice
but to let go
in order to allow a new chapter to unfold.

Sometimes, pain is a sign for the Earth to
hold you more tenderly when you take
your next step.

UNCERTAINTY IS THE ONLY CERTAINTY

"I don't know"
is a good place to be.
"I don't know" is an opening.
"I don't know" is the acceptance
that you will never know.
And when you accept that you will never know,
the weight of uncertainty and fear shifts to make
space for the state of excitement and wonder.

REMAIN SOFT LIKE WATER

When life keeps showing you the same thing over and over again, then sooner or later surrendering will happen. It will happen.

And then you will discover the outcome of not trying to fight, or resist, or change what is being shown to you. You will experience a subtle shift within your heart.

You will experience freedom.

(We make waves out of stillness to try and return to stillness.)

April Green

True stillness is found in
accepting everything that arises
so that you are soft enough to allow
everything that arises to pass
through.

April Green

RAIN AGAINST THE AIR

If we have inner agitation—desires, fears, resistance, searching, projecting—then we are never truly listening to others, never truly hearing the sound of rain against the air or the heart like the sweeping beat of the ocean. Sometimes, it feels as though all we are really doing is listening to ourselves: listening to what we want to hear, what we expect to hear, and what we think will bring us the peace and contentment we are searching for. The weight of inner pain can feel so heavy that it pulls us away from the present moment. But, when we learn to become more and more present, we begin to see that freedom from inner pain and suffering sits within the heart of each moment.

And we are that beating heart.

LET IT BE AS IT IS

Accept everything:
the way you are feeling,
the guilt, the shame, the pain.
Accept it all.
Don't try to hold it back,
or push it away, or fight with it,
as this will only serve to reinforce
the tension and pain in your heart.

Allow everything to simply be. As it is.

Everything you have ever gone through is
inviting you to discover yourself as you are
now*.*

April Green

LOTUS FLOWER

Sometimes, we prefer the certainty of our pain
rather than the thought of meeting it again.
We have become so used to it that we forget it is
the thing that is weighing us down. It becomes
who we are, and we embody it.

But, when you set an intention to sit with your pain,
an energy of warmth and well-being opens up
around you. A quality of love starts to arise;
something begins holding your space.

The pain starts unfolding like a lotus flower. Moving.
Rising. Inhaling the air as it leaves to come into its
own kind of bloom.

When you understand that pain is an intrinsic part of
living, you start to build your life from this place of
deep acceptance:

*pain will always appear in your life, but it doesn't
need to stay.*

FAITH

Faith isn't the act of thinking
and praying that something good
will happen for you.
Faith is believing that in the here and now,
everything good is already happening
for you.

April Green

THE FIGHT IS KEEPING NEGATIVE EMOTIONS ALIVE

Denying and resisting negative emotions in order to protect yourself from pain is keeping the ever-present energy of love and happiness from reaching your heart.

Allow negative emotions to arise without harming you by focusing on and absorbing yourself into the opposite of those emotions. The negative emotion will then shift and change direction on its own.

If you are sad, instead of trying to fix the sadness, or remove the sadness, allow it to simply be there. The ego will try to attach meaning to the sadness and find a solution to it. But if you simply sit with it whilst turning your attention towards the state of happiness, then the energy of sadness will start to become softer and lighter. And if happiness is too far beneath the sadness to be awakened and enlivened, then this is okay. Focus instead on gratitude. Move into nature, inhale the air, reach for the little pieces of joy until the sadness disperses and you notice the energy of well-being—your birthright—rising to the surface.

April Green

SURRENDER TO WHAT YOU DON'T KNOW

Soften into the unknown a little more.
Surrender to the idea of freedom a little more.
Have faith that the Universe is always taking care
of you.

The more faith you have, the more space you create
to bear witness to the new pearls appearing upon
the thread of your life.

BEAUTY, LOVE, AND PERFECTION

You can live in wholeness and still feel sad. You can live in wholeness and still want to experience more. You can live in wholeness and still let go of the things that are no longer serving you. You can live in wholeness and still reach and stretch and grow. Problems arise when you *search* for wholeness. For when you search for wholeness, you are denying that you are already whole. When you search for wholeness, you are identifying with the limited self (ego), which is the part of the mind that will never know wholeness because it holds an image of you as broken, unworthy, unlovable, and lacking. You are not this. You must turn away from this false identity in order to feel and see who you truly are in the now. Because the now is quite simply beauty, love, and perfection appearing in wholeness. And sadness can arise here. Unhappiness can arise here. Pain can arise here. But nothing can reach into and affect the very essence of who you are when you are anchored in the wisdom that you are already whole, and already enough.

Sometimes it feels more comfortable giving
pieces of yourself away instead of setting a
boundary.

Sometimes, it feels easier to repeat the same
thing over and over again instead of pushing through
the discomfort that transformation asks of you.

Sometimes it feels softer to abandon yourself
one last time before opening your hands and letting
someone, or something go.

Be gentle with yourself.

There is no time limit to your healing and your
growth.

DANCING IN THE RAIN

When you stop allowing circumstances to control
your life, you will start dancing in the rain instead of
shielding yourself from it.

(When you start changing the inside, the things you
have no control over on the outside become softer.)

ENOUGH

Trying to control an outcome that is out of your control puts a barrier between you and the flow of life.

The minute you stop wanting something you think will bring you happiness, and instead realise that happiness is here: in all that you already have, and all that you already are, then the thing you want, or its equivalent, will start making its way to you.

This is how it works. Truly. This is how it works.

RISING

Letting go is a shift in realisation, an acceptance that you can't change what has happened; you can only change how you are responding to what has happened.

Each time you let an emotional entanglement go, you rise in consciousness. You move into a new space and your mindset shifts. You become lighter, and happier, as you realise how trapped you were in the grip of holding on. You start expressing these changes. You start seeing the fruit of these changes. You start allowing yourself to rest, reflect, cry, stand still, and heal in this new space.

And over time, each season of shedding, and softening, and mending, and healing becomes gentler.

Because you know you will always rise.

We see on the outside
whatever is unresolved
on the inside.

REMINDER

We tenderly rise to meet life each time we change something on the inside—when we clear blocked pain, remove an old belief—we repair; we reconnect with our core.

We let go.

Softening into your heart

SOFTENING INTO YOUR HEART

The process of softening into your heart starts by understanding that you are safe here, in the present moment. And whatever pain you have gone through in the past, whatever pain you are going through right now, your heart is always with you. Reconnect with your heart. Heal your heart. Breathe, and move, and check in with your heart more often. Remind yourself that it is not always possible to be your best self, that healing takes time, that you are still learning. Use this space to get to know your heart's language. Use this space to show forgiveness to yourself. Know that you do not always need to be moving forwards. If just showing up is all you can do for yourself today, then that's okay. If you love yourself throughout the process, then you are healing. Stay kind to yourself. Be gentle.

April Green

You

Once you decide to choose yourself
after betrayal, abandonment, rejection,
the Universe meets you there.
And then everything you come into contact with
starts echoing the value, and the love
you have recognised within yourself.

(The first step to healing is choosing yourself.)

Find somewhere you feel safe,
and complete, and at peace,
and enough.

Then keep returning
until you understand that
this place is already inside you:

the destination you are drawn to
is simply bringing your true self
back to the surface.

(You are already whole.)

April Green

Being with myself
is not a place I have
always loved.
But the more
I settle here,
the more I am
learning what
unconditional love
feels like.

April Green

If the greatest gift you can give
another person
is the space to be seen and heard,
then you must find all the different
ways to give yourself this space
too.

Wherever you are right now, and whatever is on
your mind right now matters. So trust the warmth
of your deeper self to hold you as you discover
where in your present situation you need the most
strength.

(Never forget that you are worthy of being seen
and heard by the entirety of yourself.)

April Green

Each time you
soften into yourself
*(give yourself the time, the nourishment,
the tenderness)*
you are valuing yourself.

Each time you soften into yourself
you are embodying the energy of love.

(Stay here.)

April Green

JUST BREATHE

Sometimes there is a rush to find something:
*(an answer, a resolution, a relief, peace, love,
contentment)* when all you really need to do
is get still and find your next breath.

SELF-BELIEF

Self-love emerges naturally
once you start pouring the energy
you've been using to please other people,
back into yourself.

(Understand that being yourself
is the greatest gift you can give another person.)

RESHAPING THE PAST

When you can revisit your past through the lens of gratitude, your past stops having such an emotional hold over you. When you see that some of the most traumatic experiences turned out to be doorways to growth, the narrative starts to shift:

the things that were once so painful
have transformed into blessings.

REMINDER

Whatever is happening now,
no matter how difficult it may feel,
will one day turn out to be a blessing.

(You just don't know what that is yet,
and this is part of the blessing.)

April Green

YOU ARE HERE

When you are connected to yourself,
you become available for life.
You become attuned to life.
You no longer look towards externals
to make you happy; because in this space
of presence, you are already that.

Life shows up exactly as it is,
(exactly as it has always been)
and you welcome it.
It satisfies you, and you stop looking
for more.

You start loving yourself and all the mountains you
have climbed to reach where you are now.

A space of deep acceptance opens up, and you start
living from there.

April Green

A healing body is a soft body,
arching and stretching, and moving
into all the right places.

HARMONY

Each time you acknowledge the sense of well-being that comes from doing something kind for yourself, you invite a re-harmonising of energy into your awareness.

The kinder you are to yourself, the kinder you are to others, and the more you start noticing kindness shining out of everything and everyone you come into contact with.

(Kindness is a virtue that returns much more to us than we give.)

YOU ARE THE ANSWER

The reason we go over a situation in our heads,
again and again, is to try and seek relief from it.
We are looking for a clue, an answer, a resolution;
the final piece we think will give us freedom from
the pain of that situation.

But the relief can never be found in the thought, or
the mental images that are created by the thought.
The relief can only be found in the background of the
thought. In the stillness, and the silence of the
present moment. And when you return to this
space, you return to life. You become available for
inspiration, intelligence, wholeness, and
completeness to meet you there.

You become the answer.

LIVING FEARLESSLY

If you are fighting with something
from the past, or looking for an answer,
or waiting for an outcome
you will not be able to respond
fully and authentically
to what life is offering you
in the present moment.
If your inner and outer worlds are misaligned,
you will not be able to respond fully to others
and you will not be able to respond fully to yourself.
If you are feeling afraid:
if what you are attached to is under threat,
you will not respond in a way that is aligned
with your values and with what you deserve.
But when you learn to absorb yourself
into every moment—consciously, deliberately,
and fearlessly—you will be here:

standing in your truth and living in complete
harmony with this truth.

April Green

YOU ARE SAFE HERE

Remind your body that it is safe here.
A memory passing through is not a signal
to re-live the pain again.

YOU ARE EVERYTHING YOU SEE AND MORE

Nothing is lacking in the space that is you.
But, thinking about the past,
trying to change the outcome of the past,
and worrying about the future
is covering the depth of who you are and
causing you to feel as though something
is missing.

Trust that nothing is missing other than your
connection with your deeper self.

(Keep returning to this truth.)

April Green

GROWTH

Taking a break is growth, resting is growth,
and crying is growth.

When a feeling arises and you give yourself
permission to weep, you are giving the pain
behind that feeling the space to be heard,
to be felt, and to be validated.

You are softening your pain in the same way
rain softens the Earth.

Never feel ashamed for resting, and weeping, and
surrendering to the depths of your pain.

For this is self-care. This is growth.

And this is why feeling it all becomes everything that
matters the most.

April Green

Your heart doesn't want
the sharp pain of resistance.
It wants the sweet, soft beat
of acceptance.

April Green

YOU ARE ENOUGH

You are enough as you are.
If you turn away from yourself
in order to taste any kind of
external validation,
you risk falling out of alignment
with who you are,
and the journey back will be
a painful one.

Stay in your own energy field.
The right people will meet you there.

April Green

LISTENING TO GRACE

The answer arises
within a quiet mind.
It arrives when you are absorbed
in the present moment.

Always.

This is how you know
it is the right answer:

It arises from grace.

ONE

When you discover everything beautiful within you,
everything outside of you starts to reflect this.

When you discover softness within you,
everything coming towards you reaches you
gently.

When you discover love and contentment within you
everything becomes one.

The dark seasons pass by
and you see them as part of the beauty.

The light comes
and you watch it enter you
and flow out of you at the
same time.

April Green

YOUR PURPOSE

When you find your healing space
your soul will draw everything
connected to that space towards
you.

When you find your healing space
you will breathe a different air,
walk a more tender path,
embody a softer light.

When you find your healing space
guard it with love and attention,
for this healing space is who you
truly are.

This healing space is your life.

April Green

COURAGE

Courage doesn't come from resisting your fears
but from getting to know them so intimately that
you learn to welcome the messages they are
bringing you.

COME HOME TO YOURSELF

Stay close to whatever is here now—
not to your imagination,
not to the past, not to the thought of
what is going to happen next—
but with what is here, and real, right now.
Like the heat of your breath, the silence,
the space in between.
Keep returning to this place until
the energy you are holding onto
fades like the dust of a falling star.

April Green

THE LITTLE THINGS

Pay attention to the little things that keep appearing
in your life: especially the little things that trip you
up and keep you feeling stuck.
Find out why they are returning: what are they
trying to teach you? And instead of blaming
yourself, or feeling as though life is coming at you,
or pushing against you, start looking within.

Remember—we attract a reflection of how we feel
about ourselves, so find out if you are holding onto
certain beliefs about what you think you deserve.

Keep going within to discover if there are
any changes you need to make to ensure you are
attracting everything that matches the value you
have placed upon yourself.

NOTES ON ATTACHMENT

Any kind of desire formed on the basis that your happiness depends on the outcome will cause you to suffer because it is a false creation—it comes from a place outside of reality.

Any promise of a state of being that comes from something outside of your control will cause you to suffer.

Anything that has a condition attached to it, ("this needs to happen before that can happen") is out of your control, and it will start a cycle of pain and torment.

When a strong desire arises, the conditions to attaining it will attach themselves so quickly you will not always see that they come from the ego and its energy of fear and lack.

Anything that puts you in a place of lack, ("I want love because I don't feel it within myself"), will keep you in a state of lack because you receive what you feel yourself to be.

April Green

When you are attached to an outcome, you usually end up fighting your way there and crushing all the beauty and joy along the way.

A healthy desire, or a preference, is neutral and clean—it doesn't have any effect on your essential self if it doesn't happen. It is created **from** a place of love and not **towards** a place of love.

The goal is to stay unmoved. The goal is to see that you are already whole, already enough, already unconditional love, and to free yourself from anything that is blocking you from **feeling** these natural states.

Everything you have quietly desired from a place of love will appear because the energy of "needing" and "wanting" is not blocking them from appearing.

Pain will still appear in your life—you will go through pain, the people you love will go through pain, tragedy will happen, and dark seasons will come. But the pain that comes from attachment to outcomes will cease because your choices will be aligned with love.

April Green

Please remove the belief that you cannot be happy without a certain person or thing.

Set an intention to consciously connect with your deeper self.

Build a relationship with yourself first.

Know that you are worthy of the unconditional love you will find here.

Then watch how your life starts to change.

NOTHING ELSE CAN GIVE YOU WHAT YOU ALREADY ARE

Attachment is a heavy chain that binds you to a false
belief that you can't be happy without a certain
person or thing.

Each time you go into something you think will
bring you the happiness you haven't yet discovered
within yourself, you go into a void—a spiral of losing
yourself over and over again as you search outside
of yourself.

But happiness is not something that can be given
to you by anyone, or anything. It is your true nature,
it is who you already are.

So who you already are must find all the different
ways to enliven that happiness and bring it back to
the surface.

April Green

CAPTURING THE LIGHT

Healing isn't supposed to be loud.
Sometimes, it is the silence between
each breath. It is the glance towards
a different patch of sky—a distance
your eyes haven't reached for a while.
It is a longer stretch in the morning,
a softer unfolding. An awareness that
the light looks a little more golden today;
transparent, impossibly beautiful.
And how the captured dust doesn't really
fall at all—it dances, and rises, and expands
into a space that, for each tiny fragment,
must feel like eternity.

April Green

YOU ARE LOVED BECAUSE YOU ARE LOVE

Find love within yourself by trusting that
you are the energy of love.

And if you don't feel ready to believe this, then try to
love *everything*: the sunlight, the shadows, the
music, the air.

Eventually, you will see that everything you have
started to love is reflecting the love you have found
within yourself.

BE THE ENERGY OF LOVE

Whenever you have moments of peace and clarity,
you will see that your happiness is not dependent on
a specific outcome or another person. It just is.
You are quite simply the energy of love and
happiness—an imprint of grace.

The daily practice is to stay aware of this truth.
The daily practice is to disallow the mental activity
of the ego from rearing its head and destroying this
truth.

Your capacity to relax into your deeper self and
understand that there are things you will never
know, things you have yet to work out, and pain you
have yet to meet is the highest form of acceptance.

*One that will create an altered mindset that will bring
forth inner happiness.*

April Green

REMINDER

External validation
cannot bring you the peace
and happiness
that your own inner being
can give you.

THERE IS NO VOID TO FILL

Seeking external validation arises when you disconnect from yourself. Seeking external validation is an act of rejecting yourself, leaving yourself behind, and handing your power to someone else because you haven't gotten to know or accept yourself enough to trust yourself.

Not being true to yourself creates a feeling of emptiness that you believe external validation will fill. But there is no real void to fill. There is simply a misguided feeling—a false belief that something is missing, or a better version of you is waiting in an imaginary hidden place.

There is no mystery. You are here, as you are, and where you belong. Trust yourself. Trust your inner world. Validate who you truly are in silence.

April Green

Don't allow a painful season
to rob you of remembering the
things that matter the most.

April Green

It is okay
to give yourself permission
to do nothing but
make it through today.

(Your strength will return.)

Sometimes,
we cling to something,
and we run with it
without getting still
and asking our heart:

"Is this the right way?"

Get to know yourself so well
that you learn how to stay with yourself
during the times you want to run.

These are the times you need yourself
more than ever before.

AVOIDING SUFFERING CAUSES SUFFERING

Don't abandon yourself when times get tough.
Everything is temporary, including the thing you
normally turn towards to help you forget, (or help
you feel better each time you want to forget).

Nothing tastes sweeter than the experience of
your true self.

Don't deny this self, or run away from it, for this is
denying life.

Honour every choice you have made, and every step
you are taking by cultivating the courage to trust
yourself.

Start from here.

April Green

FIND OUT FOR YOURSELF WHO YOU TRULY ARE

There are parts of you
that you have locked away,
disowned,
pushed deep inside;
and nothing outside of you
can bring these parts
to the surface.

Only you can do that.

Only you can know yourself so completely
that you understand and embrace your wild and
hidden parts.

Only you can explore what it means to **be you.**

(As you are—not as you think you need to be.)

April Green

TRUST THE HIGHER SPACE

Learn to view your problems
from the place that is free of problems;
from the unchanging stillness within you.

Human nature is always in motion,
always moving, always doing, always searching.
But the space at your centre doesn't move
or change. The space at your centre is stillness;
and this is your true nature.

This is your home.

April Green

Never allow rejection to lead you
to a place of self-rejection.

(There is always a reason for heartbreak,
even when you can't see it straight away.)

April Green

CREATING A DIVINE SPACE

Sometimes we say no to something because it doesn't look like what we wanted. It doesn't arrive in the package we were expecting so we push it away without realising that it could be something we need at the exact time it is delivered to us.

But when you trust that everything happens in perfect succession, you will start noticing the synchronicities, the seamless perfection, and the spontaneity of it all.

You will start living from a divine space.

NOTES ON INTUITION

Too often, we ignore our intuition at the expense of pleasing other people, not hurting their feelings, and not making waves.

We betray ourselves each time we look for the answer outside of ourselves instead of listening to the wisdom within.

We always know the answer—we just need to work on trusting ourselves enough to stand in the answer.

When you ignore your instinct, the guiding force, the connection to your source, you end up responding from a place that has been constructed out of fear. You end up creating disharmony between what you are feeling on the inside and what you are showing on the outside.

When you go against the inner knowing, you step away from the light of awareness, (you step away from who you truly are) and you become entangled in a pattern of suffering. The answer is still whispering to you.

April Green

The answer is behind the pain you end up suffering because you didn't go with your "knowing" in the first place.

Intuition happens when your higher self sees the whole all at once—it connects everything all at once—the way a painter envisages a completed painting on an empty canvas.

When you forget this instinctive knowing—when you try to force it based on what happened in the past, or by thinking about it, constructing how you think it is going to unfold, then things will go wrong, and you will suffer.

Never abandon the feeling of inner wisdom—this is your authenticity, your power, and your faith in a higher self. Never allow the ego, the pain of the past, or the projection of an outcome to lead the way.

Your higher self always hears your deepest desires, and quietly leads the way.

Never analyse what you know to be true because you will start breaking it into pieces, and it will no longer be true. Intuition can't be limited or pulled apart.

April Green

It arrives as a single, whole, illumination guiding you in the same way streetlights guide you home. The second you doubt it, or go against it, is the moment you choose a darker path.

Intuition is alive and it is drawing you towards your greater good. When you acknowledge it and honour it, you align with it.

Never doubt the decisions you make based on a heart feeling. Don't explain your decisions either. For there is glory to be found in learning to trust how your heart is feeling. There is power to be found in listening to the awareness that arises when energy moves around your bones like a storm about to break.

Don't disrespect this energy. Teach yourself how to understand it so that you can live your life from this divine source.

April Green

WITHIN

Inner problems are not resolved by changing something on the outside. The constant fear of not being good enough, of rejection, of being hurt, will not go away by striving to look a certain way or achieve a certain thing.

Inner problems are resolved when you go within and find the part that needs to be seen, and heard, and released.

Inner problems are resolved when you fill yourself up with love and acceptance from within.

Whenever any doubt arises, call your energy
back—keep centering yourself within your own
being.

(You always instinctively know what is right for
you.)

Don't speak too much of the past:
speak of the flowers,
speak of the mercy,
speak of the love you see now;
and your delicate language will return
on the wind and
soften the weight of your pain.

April Green

Putting your energy into the past to try and find
the answer, or change the outcome, takes you away
from *being* the answer now.

(Don't turn away from the flowers already in bloom
to water the ones that have already died.)

April Green

Answers arrive in the now
and they relate to what you're going
through now.
They arrive at the exact moment
you need them.

(Create the space to hear them.)

April Green

GRATITUDE

Gratitude for having enough,
and being enough right now,
will very naturally put you into
a positive emotional state.

And, when you are grateful
for what you already have,
what you already have
starts to expand organically.

When you live in gratitude, your energy goes into
creating your present moment instead of avoiding it.

When you live in gratitude, your reactions and
responses to life arise from a place of wisdom.

When you live in gratitude, you notice flowers
lining the darkest of paths.

April Green

FORGIVENESS IS FOR YOU

The first step towards forgiveness
is making things right in your own heart
first.

It takes compassion and humility
to forgive yourself for whatever it is
you are holding against yourself.

But you must. For this is the most
important step towards opening your heart
and loving, and receiving, and giving, and
breathing—freely.

You do not deserve to carry the weight
of the past into your present moment.

Every step of your journey is sacred,
delicate, wild, and forgiving.

Allow yourself to live in harmony with
this promise.

April Green

Desires that aren't born from a place of love
are the kind of desires that bring disappointment.

Even when they are met.

When fear rises,
understand that it is usually
because you have lost touch
with yourself.

Treat fear as a message
to create some space
to invite the stillness and
the unconditional love of your
deeper self to be felt.

(Re-connect)

April Green

One day, you will be able to re-visit a painful situation and you will not react to it—your heart won't feel any pain. You will become unmoved.

Never underestimate the power of spending time alone to heal and explore what certain situations have been teaching you about yourself.

(Self-reflection is self-care.)

Softening into your power

ON BEING SOMEONE

Sometimes, it feels as though there is an everlasting struggle to become someone, to do something, or to get somewhere.

But if you could learn how to sink deep into your being—discover the hidden life, the rain gathered in your bones, the shape of the pearls—you would get to know (and accept) the most valuable parts of yourself. You would find out what living your most authentic life truly means:

loving who you already are.

April Green

WE ARE HERE

We can understand our psychological self; we can
read about boundaries, healing, patterns, conditions,
reasons, and meaning. And all of this is valuable. All
of this has led us to where we currently are. But too
much analysing can reinforce a false belief that we
are broken and can learn how to be fixed. Too much
information can turn into the construction of a false
image pressed into the air. And this is not who we
are. We are here. The one who is reading this now
is the one we must get to know. The one who is
seeing this now is the one we must get to trust. The
one who is feeling and tasting and touching is the
one who is alive in this moment. And although we
must honour our journey, and all the pain we have
endured to reach where we are now, we must not
abandon each living moment in favour of
remembering who we once were.

April Green

The purpose of life
is to enjoy it,
celebrate it,
evolve in consciousness,
and
realise your true self.

April Green

Sometimes, you just have to
rise above the noise and the chaos
and dance with grace.

(That's all she truly wants of you.)

April Green

REWILDING

When you awaken to the untamed,
boundless nature of life as it appears
in every moment—*new, and fresh,
and alive*—you will remember it
as the truth of who you are.

And when you rewild your way back
to this truth, you will see that you were
never lost at all.

You were simply living and breathing
and dancing and screaming through it
all.

April Green

Notice the way the rain falls tender and wild—we too must live the same.

LOVE YOURSELF

Your concept of yourself
determines the kind of flowers
that bloom in your life.

April Green

LIFE IS ON YOUR SIDE

There is nothing more beautiful
than experiencing life
and all it has to offer you
instead of using life to try and fix
what you think is lacking in your life.

(There is power in seeing that life is on your side.)

THE VERY ESSENCE OF STRENGTH IS VULNERABILITY

If you are betrayed by someone
after letting them in, showing them
your scars, your vulnerability, your heart;
then know that you have not betrayed yourself.

You have grown.

You have opened a new space
in your healing journey.

April Green

When you show up for yourself each day:
when you dedicate space for the little things
(the little things that offer you so much)
you are nurturing your life,
you are caring for your life.
you are grateful for your life.

You are affirming that
the best version of your life
is already yours.

I no longer spend time with someone
to make me feel more whole.
I spend time with someone
because my wholeness makes me feel
more of them.

April Green

ALIGN YOURSELF WITH WHAT IS FOR YOU

Sometimes, you will keep giving time and energy to someone you're not truly aligned with in the hope that the more you give, the more you will eventually become aligned.

But what is happening in your emotional field now? What is being revealed to you now? How are you feeling now?

If there is pain in your life from this current situation, then it is blocking your heart from opening up to receive the love you truly deserve.

(When you are waiting for something to happen, you are unconsciously rejecting your life and every gift that is trying to reach you.)

April Green

LOVE EVERYTHING

Your seeds will grow
into something
beautiful
when the intention
for planting them
comes from a place of
love.

CLARITY AND ALIGNMENT

When you have clarity
and alignment within yourself:
you know who you are,
you know what you value,
you know what you are worth,
and you are doing the daily work of
staying close to these core beliefs;
you will not be easily pulled into
a space that causes you to feel
unbalanced and confused.

When you have clarity
and alignment within yourself
your whole life falls into a very beautiful
and harmonious order.

The depth that you are
is soft and quiet; open and empty.
It is your space to fill.

Don't allow other people to interpret
your life for you.
Don't allow other people, memories, ideals,
and perceptions,
to tell you what you need.

The Universe is always guiding you:
trust it to gently move you to where you need
to be.

April Green

Quietly listening:

to what you are
observing,
to which part is
responding,
(the past, the pain, the trauma)

is self-enquiry
is self-knowledge
is self-care.

And this is your power.
This is your daily work.

April Green

RETURNING

You don't need approval or validation
to feel good about yourself.
Let go of all that is occurring on the outside,
and return to all that you are on the inside.

(Nothing should ever damage your sense of worth.)

April Green

It's okay to have moments of sadness:
to grieve and cry for the loss
of a friendship,
a lover, the good times.
But it's not okay to betray yourself
and go back when nothing has changed
other than your perception of why you
walked away in the first place.
And if there are days when you feel like
giving in, may joy find a way to reach you
and remind you how loved you already are.

(Note to self.)

The moment
you fully embrace
every piece of who you are
is the moment the Universe
creates an even greater space
for you to step into.

(Stay unapologetic about living in this space.)

April Green

YOUR POWER LIES IN KNOWING WHO YOU ARE

You can't lose who you already are.
And who you already are can't be defined
by anyone but you.
Only you can know the fullness of yourself.
And if ever you forget, then it is only you who can
push past the fear, break something open, and
immerse yourself back into your centre.

Never forget that the comfort and well-being
of your deeper self is available to you whenever you
need it.

April Green

TRANSCENDENCE

Don't pick up an old lesson and think you will get a
different result just because it has returned in a
different shape.

The reward will be shown to you once you step over
the temptation and show yourself and the Universe
how much you have grown.

(Anything that is unresolved within you
has to be resolved by you, otherwise it will keep
reappearing in your life.)

April Green

SUNRISE

The moment you acknowledge your worth
is the moment your worth rises to meet you.
And in the warmth of this sweet recognition
you become filled with the ability to hear
and act upon your deepest values.
You find your voice. You find your courage.
You reconnect with your inner warrior,
and it is confirmed:

you will never compromise your worth again.

BECOMING WILD IN MY OWN HABITAT

Days when my soul yearns to be closer
to the heart of the things I love
are the days I give myself permission
to become lost in my own space.

April Green

SELF-COMPASSION IS POWERFUL

The part of you that doesn't believe your value
is the part that still believes what others once told
you. It is the part that still identifies with how
others once made you feel.

This is the part that needs to be treated with the
most compassion and uprooted with the most care.

Understand that healing is accepting your
wholeness; and this acceptance must include the
delicate parts you don't always realise exist until
something on the outside touches them.

Be curious about the things that trigger your
deepest wounds. And instead of running from them,
understand that they are here to help you evolve
and make new connections without any further
pain.

April Green

Create sacred spaces
where you don't have to be anyone else
but yourself.

UNCONDITIONAL LOVE

The Universe is giving you exactly what you need at every moment, even though it may not feel like that, and even though you may not always like it.

Accepting what life is showing you is empowering. You don't need to give any meaning to it—even if it feels like something is being taken away—don't view it from a place of lack. Nothing that is being shown to you is produced from a place of lack, but from a place of unconditional love. Everything is for you—it is perfect.

It is opening you up to new experiences, kindred connections, and endless possibilities.

Nothing is ever truly lost.

YOU ARE ALREADY WHOLE

When you acknowledge that you are already whole, you stop making demands and setting expectations on yourself. You no longer find yourself dwelling in a place of lack, but a place of gratitude and abundance.

Your happiness no longer depends on the fulfilment of external desires but on the connection you have with your deeper self.

When you acknowledge that you are already whole, you begin to meet the Universe as one whole, and your frequency starts synchronising.

Your whole power is made available to you, and the search for better and more comes to an end.

April Green

BE WHO YOU ARE

Be who you are entirely.
Do not divide yourself into pieces—
stay grounded in your wholeness.
Explore your own experience of being yourself.
Express your shadows safely, blend them into light.
Trust the depths of your inner knowing, not the
shallow, quick-to-speak voice of doubt and shame.
Align yourself with what is true for you.
Understand that you can change and evolve in
consciousness whenever you desire.

What could be more sacred than your very own
creation when that creation is you?

April Green

LOVE WHAT YOU LOVE

When you start living consciously,
you start creating your life out of
love for your life.

Each time you choose to honour your worth,
over connections that reduce you to feeling
less than enough, your worth becomes stronger.

(And the unconditional love you have for yourself
starts to shine through.)

FINDING YOUR PURPOSE

Allow the natural flow of life
to touch you and direct you.

There is no effort once you become
divinely attuned to your heart's highest
frequency.

DO WHAT YOU LOVE FOR YOU

When creating, do it for yourself.
Do it because you love doing it.
Do it because it sustains you.
Do it because the darkness needs to speak.
Do it because your heart skips a beat.
Do it because you've been called to do it.
Do it because others may need it at the exact time
you give it away.

April Green

SOFTENING INTO YOUR POWER

Softening into your power is an act of silently
honouring your values so that when a situation
appears that could swiftly, and destructively pull
you away from those values, you are less inclined
to respond.

Softening into your power is an act of observing and
listening to what others have to say without being
moved from your place of integrity.

Softening into your power is being yourself;
showing up as you are and standing in the
awareness that you have travelled too far to ever
turn back.

April Green

THE POWER OF AFFIRMATIONS

When you unconsciously identify with not feeling good enough you attract people and situations that reinforce this belief. When you judge yourself, you think other people are judging you too. When you doubt yourself, you think other people are doubting you too. When you don't like yourself, you think other people don't like you too.

And when you become conscious that your deep-rooted beliefs are attracting the wrong things into your life, you start to heal your beliefs.

(The daily practice.)

FALL BACK INTO YOURSELF

The desire for more, and better occurs when you have walked too far from yourself. The further you walk; the more desires and demands will arise due to the mistaken belief that the fulfilment of them will bring you home.

When you start to see this cycle, you will start to understand the cause of the profound emptiness and loneliness we so often feel. You will see that the pattern of seeking pleasure and resisting pain can lead us to unhealthy behaviour in an attempt to be free of these profound feelings.

But the only way to be truly free is to fall back into yourself and see that you have no need to run from your very own beautiful habitat.

The desire for a more fulfilling and happy life is a healthy desire as long as you see that fulfilment and happiness must come from within yourself first.

CREATIVITY HEALS

Find the thing that helps you feel most aligned and nourished.

Then: let it consume you.

(Anything that no longer serves you will quietly fall away.)

INTENTION IS EVERYTHING

Desiring something from a place of love,
and desiring something because you think it will
lead to love are completely different things, and
will give you completely different outcomes.

If it doesn't feel right,
you don't have to stay.
The next step is always where
you need to be.

A true connection happens
when a person matches your energy,
not when you lower your frequency
to meet theirs.

(Don't lose yourself. Stay true to who you are
and the value you have placed upon yourself.)

April Green

We have grown too used to our lives, too
accustomed to the ordinary as we search
for the extraordinary.

But the ordinary is extraordinary
when we live in an awakened state—not from
memory or anticipation—but awake, alert,
moment by moment; within life's magical
gaze.

April Green

EMBODYING WHOLENESS

Sometimes, I have to remind myself: why does there need to be an outcome?

There should just be a thousand new moments and then a thousand more. We are too conditioned to believe that our journey needs a destination or a result before another one can begin. But there is only this one—with many different flowers and many different seasons along the way. And it is up to us to step right in and feel it all, celebrate it all: the wholeness, the wildness, the fragrance, the air; and still allow ourselves to have a fierce season, a tender season, a grounding season, and a season filled with sadness and despair. We are allowed to rise like a warrior one day and fall like a warrior the next. We are allowed to show up in whatever shape that takes, even if that shape is a stranger, a child, or a sadness we've never felt before. Because this is all part of our wholeness—this is who we truly are. So we must be brave enough to claim it. We must love ourselves enough to embody it. We must **feel** how much we matter. We must **realise** how much we belong.

April Green

RESETTING

A boundary is for you:
it is an act of self-care.

If someone doesn't respond well
to your boundary,
this is not a reflection on you,
but on their own lack of self-care.

Keep setting and resetting
your boundaries.
And, more importantly—
keep honouring them.

It is your birthright to stand up for yourself,
and express what matters to you the most.

April Green

Don't be too hard on yourself if you find
yourself entering the same season twice.
Sometimes you have to return to an old lesson
in order to close the door behind you with
a little more force.

April Green

REMINDER

The higher self looks for
beauty, peace, silence, and stillness.

The lower self (ego) looks for pleasure,
ownership, and control which takes you outside
of reality.

Anything constructed from here will not bear fruit.

Stay aligned with your true nature.

It is only an inhale away.

THE POWER OF INTEGRITY

Understand that unhealed wounds of the past are
still energetic; so if they are triggered by an external
event, they will create a storm in your bones, and a
cloud so thick and heavy that you will lose a grip on
your response.

*You hold the power to radically transform your life by
healing your deepest wounds so that you are never
moved from your place of integrity.*

REMINDER

Give yourself permission to
withdraw your energy from
anything that isn't in line with
your growth.

Something incredible happens
when you go towards fear
instead of allowing it to come
to you.

April Green

Whatever state of mind
you ask for
will always appear.

The mind is a wonderful servant;
so make sure you direct it from a place of love
and not from a place of fear.

April Green

SOFTENING INTO WHOLENESS

When you soften into your wholeness,
and accept life exactly as it is, you will see
the pain of the past dissolving into light.

Being alone is not linked
to a lower sense of worth, but to
a higher sense of knowing what
you are worth.

(When you prioritise your worth,
the right people will always find you.)

April Green

REMINDER

Inner work can be difficult and painful.

But the suffering caused by repeating
old patterns and behaviours
is soul destroying.

There is something beautifully
powerful
about welcoming what comes
without trying to change it.

April Green

Listen a little harder
to the inner call.
Lean into your purpose
a little more.

You have a gift to give the world,
and that gift is yourself.

April Green

I am already whole. I am already enough.
I am already whole. I am already enough.
I am already whole. I am already enough.
I am already whole. I am already enough.
I am already whole. I am already enough.
I am already whole. I am already enough.
I am already whole. I am already enough.
I am already whole. I am already enough.
I am already whole. I am already enough.
I am already whole. I am already enough.
I am already whole. I am already enough.
I am already whole. I am already enough.
I am already whole. I am already enough.
I am already whole. I am already enough.
I am already whole. I am already enough.
I am already whole. I am already enough.
I am already whole. I am already enough.
I am already whole. I am already enough.
I am already whole. I am already enough.
I am already whole. I am already enough.

April Green

April Green is an author from London, UK.

She is qualified in Reiki healing, and is currently training in Spiritual Life Coaching, and Positive Sobriety Coaching.

April is passionate about helping others uncover their inner wisdom, break through fear, and get back to their authentic selves.

You can connect with April and read more about healing, recovery, self-love, growth, and spiritual transformation by visiting her regular blog:

www.bloomforyourself.co.uk

Instagram, and twitter @loveaprilgreen

— acknowledgements —

Sasha, Tina, Xavier

&
a very special thank-you to my readers.

your love means more to me than you will ever
know.

CPSIA information can be obtained
at www.ICGtesting.com
Printed in the USA
LVHW010826150723
752268LV00004B/121

9 781399 937313